# A Visual Dictionary of Victorian Life

Bobbie Kalman

Crabtree Publishing Company

www.crabtreebooks.com

# Crabtree Visual Dictionaries

## Created by Bobbie Kalman

Ági és Marikának,
nagyon sok szeretettel Babitol


**Author and Editor-in-Chief**
Bobbie Kalman

**Research**
Enlynne Paterson

**Editors**
Kathy Middleton
Crystal Sikkens

**Design**
Bobbie Kalman
Katherine Berti

**Print and production coordinator**
Katherine Berti

**Prepress technician**
Katherine Berti

**Illustrations**
Illustrations by Barbara Bedell except:
Antoinette "Cookie" Bortolon: pages 1, 3 (top left), 14 (bottom left), 15 (women-top), 16 (bottom left)
Patrick Ingoldsby: pages 3 (top right), 11 (lamp)
Janet Kimantas: front cover (house), pages 7 (top right), 8 (bottom)
Trevor Morgan: page 8 (middle left)
Bonna Rouse: pages 16 (man-top center), 19 (girl sewing), 27 (bottom right), 29 (middle right)
Hilary Sandham: page 15 (girl in reefer jacket)

**Photographs and reproductions**
Circa Art: pages 18 (bottom right), 24 (bottom right), 27 (top right and bottom left), 28 (bottom left), 30 (bottom), 31 (top right)
Harpers Weekly: page 27 (top left)
Photos.com: pages 4, 5 (top), 10 (bottom), 18 (top left), 29 (top)
Wikipedia: Sir George Hayter: page 5 (bottom); Pierre-Auguste Renoir: Girls at the Piano: page 24 (top left); Mary Cassatt: page 31 (top left); Cornelius Krieghoff: page 31 (bottom left); John Everett Millais: page 31 (bottom right)
Other photographs and reproductions by Shutterstock

**Library and Archives Canada Cataloguing in Publication**

Kalman, Bobbie, 1947-
A visual dictionary of Victorian life / Bobbie Kalman.

(Crabtree visual dictionaries)
Includes index.
ISBN 978-0-7787-3507-6 (bound).--ISBN 978-0-7787-3527-4 (pbk.)

1. Canada--Social life and customs--19th century--Dictionaries, Juvenile. 2. United States--Social life and customs--19th century--Dictionaries, juvenile. 3. Canada--Social life and customs--19th century--Pictorial works--Juvenile literature. 4. United States--Social life and customs--19th century--Pictorial works--Juvenile literature. 5. Picture dictionaries--Juvenile literature. I. Title. II. Series: Kalman, Bobbie, 1947- . Crabtree visual dictionaries.

FC88.K365 2011 j971.0403 C2011-900072-5

**Library of Congress Cataloging-in-Publication Data**

Kalman, Bobbie.
A visual dictionary of Victorian life / Bobbie Kalman.
p. cm. -- (Crabtree visual dictionaries)
Includes index.
ISBN 978-0-7787-3507-6 (reinforced library binding : alk. paper) -- ISBN 978-0-7787-3527-4 (pbk. : alk. paper) -- ISBN 978-1-4271-9475-6 (electronic (pdf))
1. United States--Social life and customs--19th century--Pictorial works--Juvenile literature. 2. Canada--Social life and customs--19th century--Pictorial works--Juvenile literature. 3. Dwellings--United States--History--19th century--Pictorial works--Juvenile literature. 4. Dwellings--Canada--History--19th century--Pictorial works--Juvenile literature. 5. Material culture--United States--History--19th century--Pictorial works--Juvenile literature. 6. Material culture--Canada--History--19th century--Pictorial works--Juvenile literature. 7. Picture dictionaries--Juvenile literature. I. Title. II. Series.

E661.K215 2011
973.6--dc22

2010052194

**Crabtree Publishing Company**

www.crabtreebooks.com 1-800-387-7650

Printed in the U.S.A./022011/CJ20101228





**Published in Canada**
**Crabtree Publishing**
616 Welland Ave.
St. Catharines, Ontario
L2M 5V6

**Published in the United States**
**Crabtree Publishing**
PMB 59051
350 Fifth Avenue, 59th Floor
New York, New York 10118

**Published in the United Kingdom**
**Crabtree Publishing**
Maritime House
Basin Road North, Hove
BN41 1WR

**Published in Australia**
**Crabtree Publishing**
386 Mt. Alexander Rd.
Ascot Vale (Melbourne)
VIC 3032

# Contents

# The Victorian era

The Victorian **era**, or period of time, was between the years 1837 to 1901, when Queen Victoria ruled Britain. In the United States and Canada, many changes took place during this time. Many people **immigrated** to North America to start new lives. People moved into cities to work in the factories. Some people became very wealthy and had beautifully decorated homes. The word "Victorian" stood for fancy homes, fancy furniture, fancy clothes, and new ways to travel. It also meant better lives for children.

## Victoria and Albert

Queen Victoria married her German cousin Prince Albert in 1840. Victoria gave birth to nine children. She and Albert loved their children and gave them a lot of attention. The couple was very popular around the world, and people everywhere imitated the things they did. For example, Prince Albert brought the custom of decorating Christmas trees from Germany to England. People in North America soon started the custom, as well (see pages 22–23).

*The picture on the left shows Queen Victoria and Prince Albert on horseback. Below is their wedding day. They were married for 21 years, until Albert died in 1861. Victoria then moved into her castle in Scotland and did not see visitors after that. She died in 1901 at the age of 82. Her birthday is celebrated as a holiday in Canada each May.*

# Fancy homes

In North America, people built Victorian-style homes because it made them feel rich and successful. Even the **settlers** who lived in the new towns of the West built Victorian homes. Living in a Victorian home made life in a new place seem more like the old way of life people left behind. Some Victorian homes were small, but most were two or three stories high. Houses were built of brick, wood, or stone. Victorian homes were very fancy—both on the outside and inside. They looked like dollhouses. People paid a great deal of attention to detail when they built them. Some were painted in several colors. People still live in the Victorian homes built long ago, and the Victorian style is popular for new homes being built today.

*This two-story Victorian home was built of brick. It is made up of many shapes. Find four or more shapes used. The home has* ***wraparound porches****,* ***turrets****, and* ***gables****.*

*A turret is a small tower. This house has two turrets.*

*A porch is a sheltered area on the outside of a home. A wraparound porch surrounds part of a home.*

*wraparound porches*

*A gable is a triangular decoration over a window or door.*

*Victorian homes that are painted in three or more colors are called* ***painted ladies****. Name the colors used on the homes below and on the home on the right.*

*Some Victorian homes have one or more turrets on their steep, pointed roofs. How many turrets can you count on these two pages?*

*Some Victorian homes have steep, pointed roofs.*

*Victorian homes often have steep roofs with many gables facing in different directions. How many gables can you see on this home?*

*Some Victorian homes have* ***stained-glass*** *windows like this one. Stained glass is colored glass with designs on it.*

*This home is called the Wedding Cake House. It is covered in trim called* ***gingerbread trim****. How is this home like a cake?*

# Victorian kitchens

The kitchens in early Victorian homes were located either in the basement or on the first floor. Early homes had fireplaces for cooking food. In later homes, the fireplace was replaced by one or more stoves. The family on the right is cooking their meal over a fireplace. They are using a **bread oven** for baking bread and cakes.

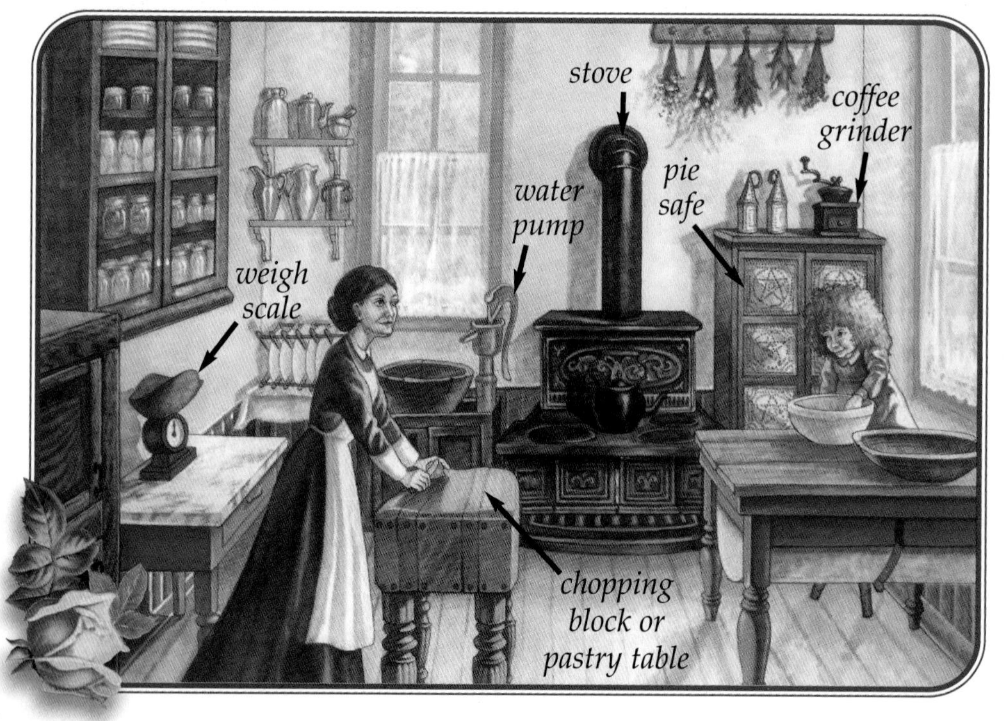


*(left) This mother and her daughter are cooking in a later Victorian kitchen. Instead of a fireplace, they cook their food on a stove.*

*These are some of the items that could be found in a Victorian kitchen:*

- *stove*
- *water pump*
- ***pastry** table/chopping block*
- *pie safe (where pies and cakes were kept)*
- *weigh scale*
- ***coffee grinder***

*Find them in this kitchen.*

## Cooking and cleaning

Many families hired servants to do most of the cooking and cleaning in their homes. The **scullery**, shown on the right, was the workroom where supplies were kept and where servants washed dishes and polished the silver and brass.

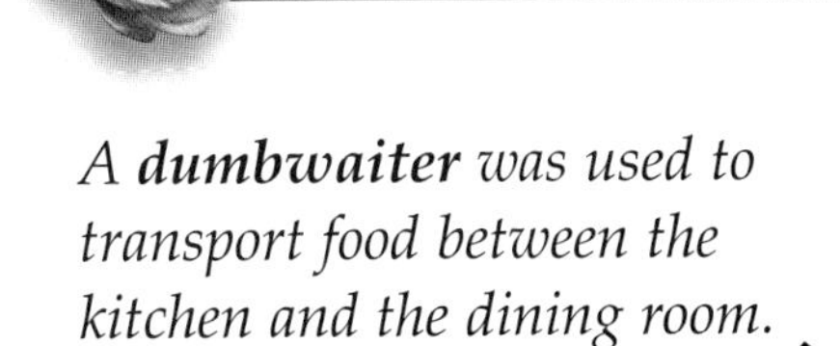

*A **dumbwaiter** was used to transport food between the kitchen and the dining room.*

*Family members used a **call box** to call their servants. When someone needed a servant, he or she pulled the knob or sash that was connected to the call box. A bell rang, and a number popped up on the box, telling in which room a servant was needed.*

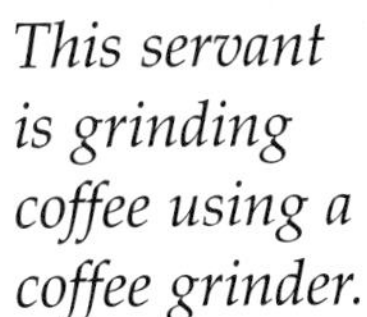

*This servant is grinding coffee using a coffee grinder.*

# What is a parlor?

The **parlor** was the fanciest and most formal room in the Victorian home. It was also called the **salon** or **drawing room**. A parlor was decorated in dark, rich colors, such as navy blue, burgundy, gold, and dark green. It was crowded with fancy furniture to show a family's wealth. Heavy curtains and stained-glass windows kept out sunlight. Sunlight would have faded the colors of the furniture. On Sundays, families gathered in the parlor to read, talk, play the piano, or entertain guests. Guests were usually invited into the parlor.

*This large family is spending Sunday afternoon in the parlor. Grandmother and Grandfather have come to visit. The children are dressed in their best clothes. Two are playing a game on the floor. One of the girls is looking after the baby. What are the other people doing?*

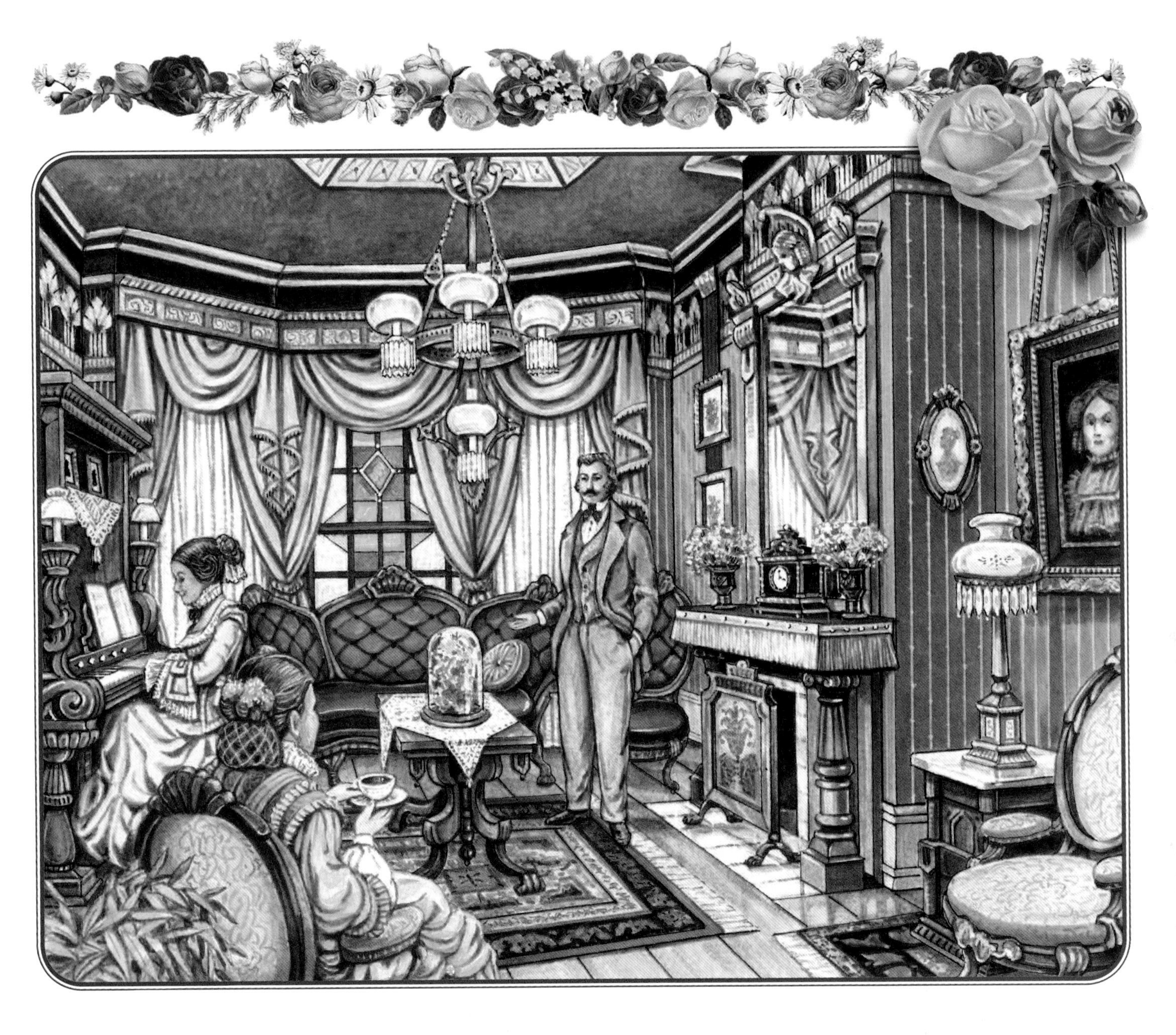

## A scavenger hunt

The parlor above has a lot of furniture and other items. Go on a **scavenger hunt** in this parlor and find items that are like the ones in these pictures.

*picture in frame*

*clock*

*lamp*

*chair*

*mirror*

*teacup and saucer*

# Bed and bath

**Bed chambers**, or bedrooms, were on the second floor of the house. They were very private and never seen by guests. Besides sleeping, bed chambers were also used for sewing, reading, and relaxing. Victorian homes did not have closets. Clothes were stored in drawers or cabinets called **wardrobes**. Bedrooms had fireplaces because there was no **central heating** in those days. With central heating, the whole house is heated by a furnace, usually in a basement.

*Early homes did not have running water, so people used a **washstand** to keep clean. A washstand contained a basin, pitcher of water, soap, washcloths, and towels.*

*Look at all the things in this bedroom. There is a **four-poster bed**, washstand, **chamber pot**, chest of drawers, wardrobe, comfortable chair, **chaise lounge**, and tables. Name some other items in the room.*

## The water closet

People did not bathe very often during the Victorian era. To take a bath, people had to heat water on a stove and carry it up to the second floor. It took a long time to heat enough water for a bath! Those who could afford it, added **water closets** to their homes, like the one shown below. People were shy about having them, so they hid the sinks, bathtubs, and toilets in cabinets and behind stained glass or curtains. When **indoor plumbing** became available, people could flush toilets. They could also fill bathtubs by turning on a faucet. Not many people, however, could afford indoor plumbing!

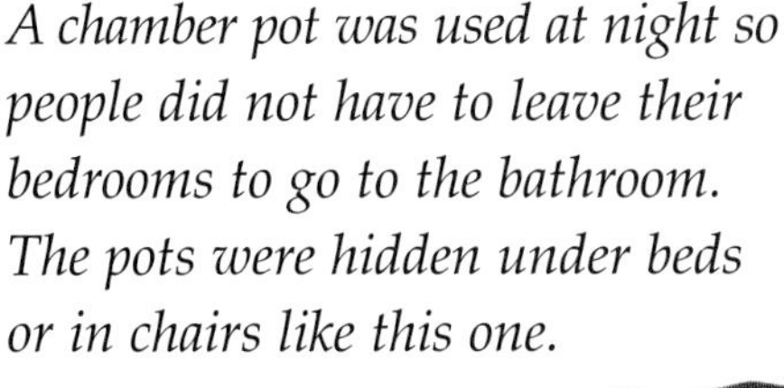

*A chamber pot was used at night so people did not have to leave their bedrooms to go to the bathroom. The pots were hidden under beds or in chairs like this one.*

*This bathtub looks more like a cabinet than a tub!*

*Later bathtubs looked more like this, but few were covered in gold the way this one is.*

# Female fashions

The clothing worn during Victorian times depended on where someone lived. Many people were farmers and wore clothing that was comfortable and plain. On Sundays and special occasions, people wore their best clothes. Those who were wealthy dressed in fancy clothes. "Fancy" is the word that best describes Victorian fashions.

*Some fancy dresses were very tight. Women had trouble walking in them.*

*Everyday clothes for most women were long dresses, aprons, and bonnets.*

*Most children had two sets of clothes. They wore one set six days a week. Their* ***Sunday-best*** *clothes were worn to church and to visit friends and family. Children were not allowed to play in these good clothes.*

*Babies and toddlers wore soft* ***bonnets*** *decorated with ruffles.*

*Large straw hats decorated with bows, feathers, and flowers were worn during the middle 1800s.*

*Straw hats were popular summer hats for boys and girls.*

*The poke bonnet had a large, stiff brim that nearly "poked" nearby people in the eye!*

*In the 1850s, women wore dresses with* ***crinolines*** *underneath. The crinoline gave a dress a hoop shape.*

***Bustles*** *replaced crinolines after 1870. Bustles made skirts stand out at the back.*

*This girl and the woman above are wearing dresses with bustles.*

*Clothing became more comfortable near the end of the Victorian era. Women wore baggy pants called* ***bloomers*** *when they rode bicycles.*

*This girl is wearing a* ***reefer jacket****, which has a large collar and metal buttons.*

*Girls and women carried* ***parasols****, or light umbrellas, to shade their faces from the sun.*

# Clothes for men and boys

Farmers who worked in the fields wore linen shirts and overalls. Big straw hats protected their heads and faces from the sun.

As with women, the clothing of men depended on where the men lived, what kind of work they did, and how much money they had. Men's fashions did not change very much, however, during Victorian times. A man's suit was made up of **trousers**, or long pants, a **waistcoat**, or vest, and a coat. The main difference was how the coats were styled, how long they were, and how they were worn. Boys wore pants and shirts like those of their fathers, but some wore fancy suits that their fathers would not have worn.

*On Sundays, men wore suits with long pants, jackets, and vests.*

*This long suit coat was called a* ***frock coat****.*

*Many men wore* ***top hats*** *and* ***cravats****. A top hat is a tall, round hat with a short brim. A cravat is a short scarf tucked into or around a shirt collar.*

*The* ***Norfolk jacket*** *was a short, belted, sporty coat.*

*For outdoor activities, men wore casual clothes such as sweaters and caps.*

*The* ***box coat*** *resembled the suit jackets of today.*

*This boy's suit looked like the suit worn by his father. It had a vest, jacket, and trousers.*

***Highland costumes** were worn by Queen Victoria's sons. In the 1850s, they became popular in North America, as well.*

*Knee-length pants for boys were called **knickerbockers**, or knickers, for short. This boy is also wearing a Norfolk jacket.*

*A **sailor suit** and straw hat was a very popular outfit worn by young boys.*

*In the 1860s, short, collarless **zouave jackets** became popular. Boys wore the short braid-trimmed jacket with knickers. The knickers were also decorated with braid.*

braid

*In 1886, Frances Hodgson Burnett wrote a children's book called **Little Lord Fauntleroy**. The story—and the suit worn by the main character—were an instant success. The Fauntleroy suit had knickers and a tight, black velvet shirt with a white lace collar and cuffs. Long curly hair completed the look. Few boys could imagine a fate worse than being made to look like Little Lord Fauntleroy. Not only was it difficult to run and play in the suit, but the long curly hair was downright embarrassing! Has your mother ever made you wear something that embarrassed you? What was it?*

# Victorian children

*Queen Victoria's family*

Until the early 1800s, parents believed that children would become spoiled if they received too much love and attention. Queen Victoria helped change these beliefs. She and her husband showed their children a lot of love and paid attention to them. Other parents soon started to imitate the ways of the royal family and showed more interest in their children.

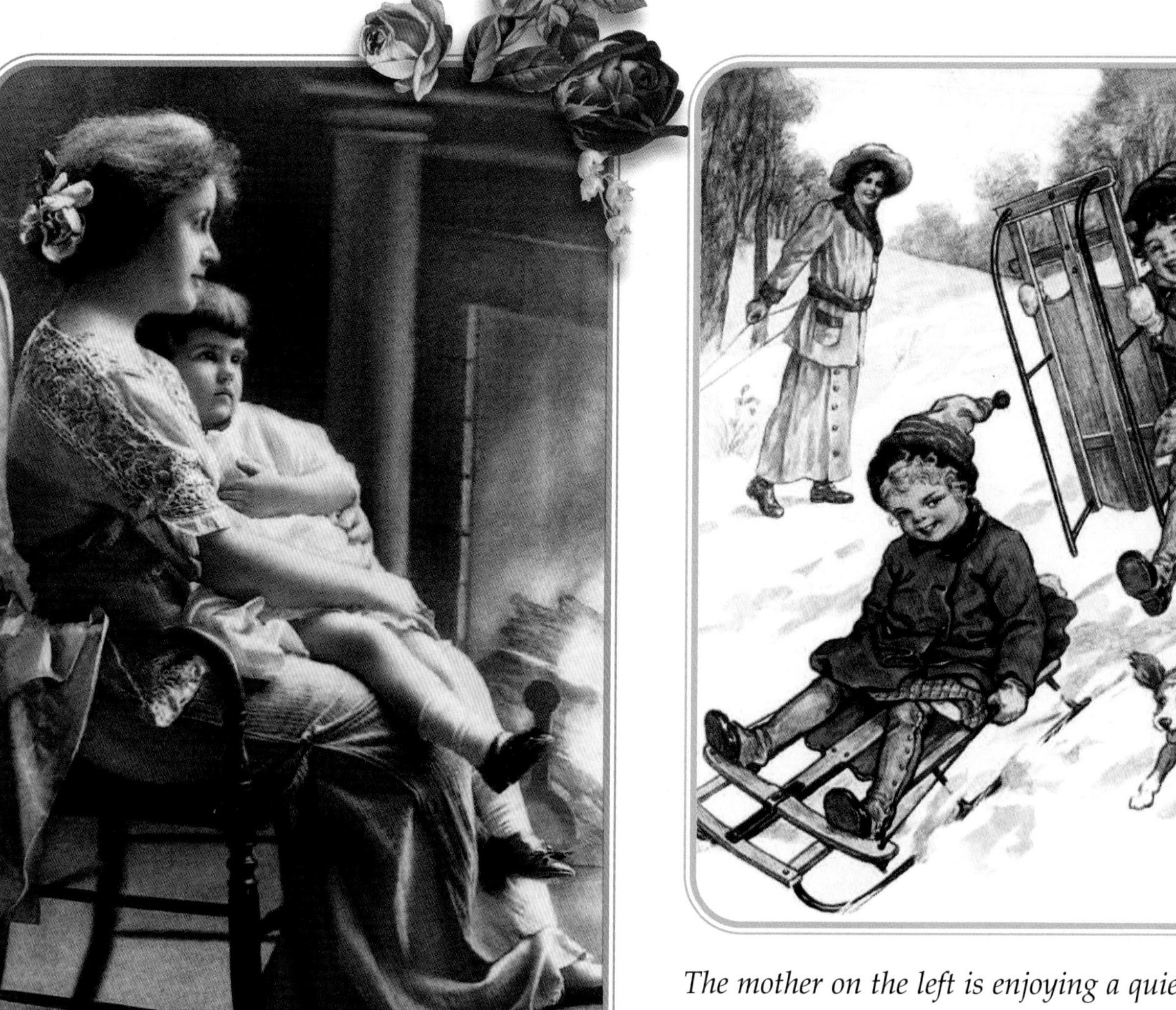

*The mother on the left is enjoying a quiet moment with her child before bedtime. The mother above is having fun in the snow with her two daughters.*

*Not all children were lucky enough to go to school. In some villages and towns there were* ***one-room schools****, where children of all ages were taught by one teacher.*

*Most children went to church on Sundays and said prayers every day. These girls are at church with their mother. They are singing religious songs called* ***hymns****.*

*Girls learned how to sew and cook from their mothers. They were expected to become wives and mothers when they grew up.*

*Many farm children had to help their parents work in the fields and look after the farm animals.*

*Some boys learned* ***trades****, such as working with wood.*

# Games and toys

During Victorian times there was no television. There were no video games or computers, but there were always people ready to play games. Families were large. Parents, several children, as well as an aunt, uncle, or grandparent sometimes lived under one roof. Children also played games at school, in the village, and at parties. Most children had very few toys. Instead, they used their imagination to create games from simple objects they found, such as old wagon wheels, hoops, sticks, pieces of rope, and snow.

*The game of Graces was played by girls. Girls used sticks to toss a hoop to each other. Catching the hoop on the stick was difficult.*

*Girls used old ropes to play skipping games.*

*Boys used them to play Tug of War.*

*Noah's Ark was the only toy children were allowed to play with on Sundays because the toy was based on a **Bible** story.*

*Children enjoyed playing outdoors. In winter, they built snowmen, went skating and sledding, and had snowball fights. They did not need toys to play with. They had one another.*

*In the late 1800s, toys were made in factories. More toys were available at cheaper prices for parents to buy.*

# Victorian Christmas

In the early 1800s, people in North America celebrated Christmas by going to church and eating a special meal with family. Queen Victoria's husband Prince Albert brought the custom of decorating a Christmas tree from his homeland, Germany, to England. People in North America quickly adopted this Christmas custom.

*(right) This picture came from a story written by an early settler. She dreamt that angels dressed in blanket coats set up a Christmas tree outside her home in the wilderness.*

*(below) Later Christmas trees were much fancier than the earlier ones. Year after year, more decorations were added. The tree was showered with candles and* ***miniature****, or tiny, furniture, musical instruments, dolls, toys, fans, stockings, and books. In most homes, the Christmas tree was the best present of all!*

# Victorian fun

Victorian people knew how to have fun. Many Victorian homes had either a piano or an organ. People made their own music. When someone played an instrument, people gathered around and sang songs together. Wealthy women spent most of their time planning and attending fancy parties. People who could not afford fancy parties held work parties, instead. Work parties were called **bees**. There were bees for husking corn, making quilts, peeling apples, and building barns. A big part of a bee was eating, dancing, and playing games. Work was fun when it was done with friends.

*At a corn-husking bee, a young man who found a red ear of corn could kiss the young woman closest to him. Will this woman let the man kiss her?*

*On summer days, people went on picnics in parks beside rivers or lakes. They dressed in their Sunday-best clothes and ate from fancy dishes.*

*After a wedding, groups of young men dressed in costumes made up of funny hats and masks, came to the home of the newlywed couple. They made "music" with cowbells, horns, and pots and pans. This wedding custom was called **charivari** or **shivaree**. Sometimes the charivari pranksters got carried away and played tricks, such as pouring water on the groom. The bride stayed inside when she saw what was happening.*

*On summer Sundays, city people crowded into carriages and went for rides in the countryside. They enjoyed getting away from busy city life.*

*People loved going for sleigh rides in winter. They kept warm underneath fur blankets. Some also placed **foot warmers** on the floor to keep warm. Foot warmers were metal boxes that contained hot coals.*

# Life in the busy cities

During the Victorian era, many young people from farms moved to the cities to work in factories. It was not easy to get jobs, however, because machines were being invented that did the jobs of people. Some families could not earn enough money for food or rent. While the poor got poorer, the rich got richer. Wealthy families lived in style. Servants took care of their homes. Some of the servants were young children who had to work to help support their families. Even though there were many problems, people found cities exciting places to live. There were parks, zoos, theaters, and interesting people to meet.

*Streets were lined with shops and people. Wagons and carriages pulled by horses took people from place to place. Streetcars were also pulled by horses. They traveled along tracks.*

*Street musicians hoped people would give them money for playing music.*

*Cities had many shops, such as this dress shop, which made and sold the latest fashions for women.*

*Wealthy city people went to the theater, opera, and to huge dance parties called balls. They dressed in their finest clothes.*

*In the middle and late 1800s, towns and cities were being built in the western parts of North America. Many people moved there to start new lives.*

# Many ways to travel

*__Penny farthings__ were the first bicycles. People began using them in the late 1800s.*

Until the middle of the 1800s, there were very few ways of getting from place to place. On land, horses pulled wagons, carriages, and coaches. On water, people paddled canoes, rowed boats, or sailed using wind power. In winter, people were able to glide over the snow on sleighs pulled by horses. People visited family and friends during this time because traveling on snow was much easier than traveling on rough roads. When trains were invented, more people traveled west to start new lives. Trains also allowed people to transport goods from the cities in the east to towns in the west. Trains helped businesses grow.

*__Hansom cabs__ were early taxis. They were named after their designer, Joseph Hansom.*

*This city couple is traveling in a fine carriage. The carriage is pulled by horses.*

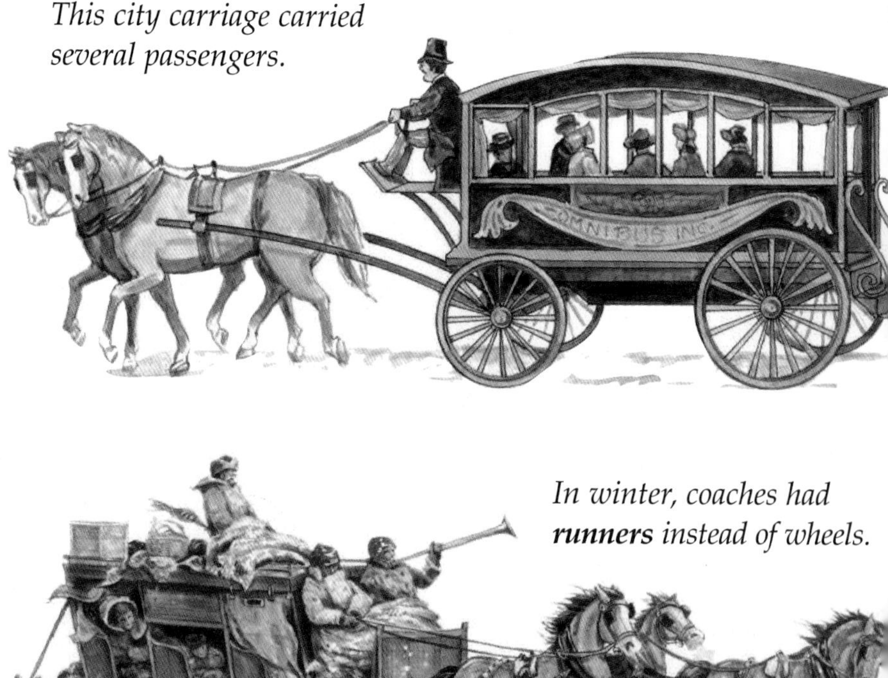

*This city carriage carried several passengers.*

*In winter, coaches had __runners__ instead of wheels.*

**Locomotives** *were built in the early 1800s and were soon used to pull train cars carrying goods and passengers. Trains became very popular because they provided a fast way to travel all around North America, allowing people to settle in new areas.*

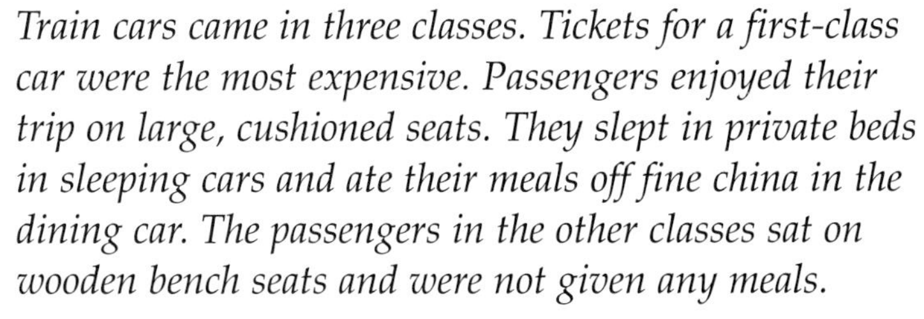

*Train cars came in three classes. Tickets for a first-class car were the most expensive. Passengers enjoyed their trip on large, cushioned seats. They slept in private beds in sleeping cars and ate their meals off fine china in the dining car. The passengers in the other classes sat on wooden bench seats and were not given any meals.*

*Luxurious steamboats made long journeys comfortable. Passengers were entertained by musicians. Steamboats also transported goods, such as cotton, sugar, and animals, to other cities.*

# Victorian art

Many famous artists lived during the Victorian era. They lived in different places and painted in different styles. Some of the most beautiful pictures were painted during Victorian times. Which of these works of art is your favorite?

*John Singer Sargent painted this beautiful picture in 1885-1886. He called it* ***Carnation, Lily, Lily, Rose*** *after a popular song at the time. He painted the picture many times to try to capture the right colors at sunset.*

(top left) This picture, called ***Girl Arranging Her Hair***, was painted by American artist Mary Cassatt in 1886. (above) One of Canada's most popular painters is Cornelius Krieghoff. He painted pictures of life in Quebec. ***The Blacksmith's Shop***, was painted in 1871. (right top and bottom) These pictures were painted by Sir John Everett Millais, a British painter. The top picture, is called ***Autumn Leaves***. The one below it is called ***The Blind Girl***. Both were painted around 1855–56.

# Glossary

**Note**: Many boldfaced words are defined where they appear in the book or are shown by pictures that are labeled.

**bee** A gathering of people that combines work with fun

**Bible** A book containing the sacred writings of the Jewish and Christian religions

**gingerbread trim** Fancy woodwork that decorated Victorian homes

**hymns** Songs of praise to God

**immigrate** To move to another country to make a home there

**indoor plumbing** A series of pipes that brings fresh water into a house and takes waste water away

**one-room schools** Schools in which children of all ages studied together in a single classroom and were taught by one teacher

**pastry** Baked goods made with dough or crust

**runners** The long metal blades on the bottom of a sleigh that glide over snow

**scavenger hunt** The search for objects hidden in a certain area

**settler** A person who makes his or her new home in a new country or a part of a country that is not yet developed

**trade** Work that requires manual or mechanical skill

# Index